Copyright @ 2020 by Michelle Owusu–Hemeng

This book is dedicated to African–

American children everywhere. You

all are wonderfully and fearfully

made.

#BlackBoyJoy

#BlackGirlMagic

We are not in darkness.

We are not savages.

We are not afraid.

We are the light.

We are the future.

We are here !

We are not out of tune.

We go with our own melody.

We are musicians.

We are the composers.

We are the culture.

We are not a harmful.

We are not a threat.

Our skin is not a weapon.

We are an investment.

Our melanin is powerful and magical.

We are not average.

We go above and beyond to

always be the best.

We are innovators.

We create new ways to make

the world a better place

We are not just kids.

We deserve to be heard.

We are inventors.

Our creations build

tomorrow's leaders.

We are not invisible.

Open your eyes and see the

potential we bring.

We are invincible.

We help save the world by

spreading love instead of hate.

We are not alone.

We work together and make things happen.

We are leaders!

We are influential.

We are the inspiration.

We are not poor.

We are rich!

We are blessed from passed generations

of inheriting becoming kings and queens.

We will continue our history of scholars.

We will stand on what is right.

We are the artist !

We will continue to be the creators

of our future.

We are not defined by what others see us as,

we define ourselves.

We are the future and our voice will always be heard.

So, Get up! Stand Tall! Speak out !

Daily Reminders

We are smart !

We are brave !

We are leaders!

We are kind !

We believe in ourselves !

We are enough!

Meet the author

Michelle Owusu–Hemeng was born in Fort Worth, Texas and raised in Arlington, Texas. She is the youngest of three. When she is not teaching she spends her time volunteering at her local orphanage. She is an advocate for social justice, quality early care and education, where she focuses on creating awareness, building support, working on change, developing professionalism, promoting child and family issues, and informing public policy.

CPSIA information can be obtained
at www.ICGtesting.com
Printed in the USA
BVHW021049020221
599223BV00021B/1055